ACCORDING TO CUSTOM

According to Custom

EAMON KELLY

MERCIER PRESS

Mercier Press
PO Box 5 5 French Church Street Cork
16 Hume Street Dublin 2

First published 1986
This impression 1995

A CIP record for this book is available from the British Library.

ISBN 1 85635 112 2

According to Custom was written for the stage by Eamon Kelly and was first presented under the title *The Story Goes* by The Abbey Theatre at The Peacock Theatre on 3 July 1979. It was directed by Michael Colgan.

Cover design by Niamh Sharkey
Printed in Ireland by ColourBooks Baldoyle Dublin 13

Contents

Introduction

In Ireland today, as in many old civilisations, it may well be said that there are three codes of law, the law of the land, the law of the church and the law of the people. When all three codes are congruent there is harmony, but where there is conflict, secret drama is born.

It is with custom as the law of the people that Eamon Kelly is concerned in his latest presentation. To material which was part of his boyhood experience in Kerry, he applies his considerable imaginative skill. True, he had to leave to see matters objectively and to realise the importance of simple phenomena and to reveal the story they tell.

To offer a simple example, when the old people greeted a sneeze (and not a cough) with *Dia linn* ('God be with us!') to have it answered with *Dia linn is Muire* ('God be with us, and Mary'), they were seeking to ward off the onset of an olden and forgotten plague of which sneezing was the prime symptom.

Even today in the Irish countryside, simple gestures are reminiscent of half-remembered rituals in which, at times the old gods war with the one god and the forces of good war with the forces of evil. These rituals tend to surface on occasions of tension like weddings, funerals or births.

When chided about these superstitions or *piseoga* the people murmur, ''Tis the custom,' or 'Don't break laws nor make laws!' And it is a brave man indeed who would defy them 'beyond the teeth'. Not all are redolent of evil – many of the customs are humorous or winsome and vouch for an admirable vein in tradition. And many of course spring from Christian sources.

On a bitter night of piled snow I was present at an Eamon Kelly show in St John's, the capital of Newfoundland. In the crowded hall were descendants of Irish cod-fishers of the 1790s, but my attention was focused on a group of Eskimoes, young men and young women, probably the pioneers of their race to be admitted to University education. Their faces were framed by hoods of spikey fur such as is seen in so many illustrations. I kept wondering how on earth these people would respond to the thoroughly indigenous Irish humour of Eamon Kelly's show. Was the cultural gap so wide that it could not be bridged?

Ten minutes of the presentation went by with the majority of the audience responding with roars of laughter or stilling to silence at a portrayal of pathos. Meanwhile, the row of Eskimoes sat gravely, uncomprehendingly gazing up at the stage as if Eamon Kelly had descended from another planet.

Then, wholly unexpectedly, on some throwaway line or gesture that eluded me, which perhaps had enabled each young Eskimo to recognise the idiosyncracies of an old man of his native village, the group broke into almost uncontrollable laughter. Later they fell silent and their eyes glistened when death was portrayed. Thus were the boundaries of time, space and race transcended by a fine artist.

Bryan MacMahon

The Dear Departed

Two priests home on holidays from the Jesuit College called into Hopper Dan's. Hopper's wife having nothing inside for the dinner – it was like her – killed two young cocks – they had hardly the red combs up on them – and put them down in the pot. She gave a bit of cold bacon to Hopper. After the dinner when Hopper was conveying the two clergymen out the yard, the old cock stretching himself to his full height and flapping his wings began to crow on the gate pier.

'That's a very proud rooster you have there!' says one of the priests to Hopper.

'No bloody wonder he would,' says Hopper, 'and he having two sons in the Jesuits!'

If you look out that window and up the rising ground towards the foot of the hills you'll see a house, and when I was a small boy there were two brothers living there. Fine storytellers they were, for what one'd leave out the other one'd put in. And signs by it was a great rambling house, with not enough chairs in the kitchen for the crowd every night. A place where the affairs of the day were debated, where entertainment mingled with education, and where what you heard was genuine, for those two brothers knew their history. A man said to me there on that floor:

'Look, Ned Kelly, there are professors above in

the University of Cork and if they had half their knowledge the devil in hell wouldn't stand them!'

But the wise are sometimes foolish. The younger brother got married when he was about thirty, but whatever he did or didn't do the wife stayed with him only one night. She ran away and if he shook gold under her feet she wouldn't come back to him. The subject was never mentioned between the two brothers until about fifty years after. The older man that never got married was complaining of a pain in his back, and the matrimonial brother getting tired of listening to him said:

'What cnavshawling have you? Hadn't you your day!'

'I had,' says the older man, 'and you had your night!'

The people living up there are still talking about the row this remark gave rise to. The two brothers could be heard shouting in the *Domhan Thoir!* When things subsided there was silence, a long silence, for they never spoke to each other after, nor did one ever again mention the other by name. When they were high over eighty and very crotchety, two men were coming home from work in Kenmare's Demesne, and when they were passing the house the younger brother came to the door and said:

'Lads, if ye'r coming over rambling tonight bring a few chairs there's one of us dead!'

That was Saturday, and an awful awkward day to die at that time, for you couldn't open a grave on Monday. Nothing but bad luck would come out of it. Of course you can get round the *piseog* by turning one sod of the grave on Sunday. And that is what was done. Only those closely connected with the dead man's family would open the grave, or be in any position of prominance during the wake or funeral. It would be considered highly disrespectful to the dead for a stranger to have hand, act or part in the proceedings.

Molly Donovan that used to lay them out when I was small, she was also the midwife. I remember seeing her up in the middle gallery of the chapel when she was old and doting, and looking down on the people coming into Mass she said:

'God made ye but it was I brought ye into the world!'

She did, and helped them out of it. The poor man that died was hardly inside the Golden Gates above when Molly was in the door and fortified with whiskey, she'd wash the corpse, put on the habit, put the pennies on the eyelids, the prayer book under the jaw and fold the arms with the rosary beads entwined around the fingers. The only case where she might look for assistance was the shaving. And a fellow helping her out one time had a ferocious shake in his hand. He was full of apologies after for not having the corpse look his best.

'Yerra,' says Molly dusting the badly shaven face with flour, 'he's all right. He'll do. It isn't to America he's going.'

Give Molly Donovan her due she carried out everything according to custom. The clock was stopped and the looking glass turned to the wall. The sad news was told to the bees, and in some places a crape was hung on the hive. Bees were considered part of the family that time and they should be told what was going on – not every fiddle-faddle, important things like the first day the child'd go to school. That morning the father'd go out and knock on the hive and say:

'Michael is gone to school today, bees.'

When Molly Donovan had the bed draped with starched linen, brought up over the foot and the head of the bed, a couple of boards under the corpse to keep him well *os cionn cláir*, his Third Order habit on him with the white cord, and he nicely groomed and serene for himself no Pope that was ever laid out in the Vatican would look half as well. Of course we didn't have the custom here of tapping him on the head with a hammer to see if he was dead!

There was a woman died east here the road. Ah she was no great loss. She made her husband's life a misery – they say she was years older than him. And when she died he spared no money on whiskey and porter for the wake. He expected to get married soon again! The drink flowed and the carpenter was so spifflicated when he came to measure the corpse he made the coffin too short. The people, when they saw the coffin going into the house the morning of the funeral, knew it was too short.

'You'd want to be blind,' they said, 'not to see that she wouldn't go into it.'

Well, the carpenter brought the coffin into the wake room, and he wanted three chairs to lay it on while he was putting the corpse into it. Of course all the chairs were below in the kitchen where the hilarity was. And the carpenter putting his head down the room door said:

'Three chairs for the corpse!'

And one blackguard below said: 'Hip! Hip!'

The carpenter laid the coffin on the three chairs and took off the lid but the corpse would not go into it! He was in an awful way now and he got very red in the face. What was he going to do? The yard full of people waiting for the funeral, the parish priest and all there. He had to act quick, so he got a lock-saw and he cut two holes at the narrow end of the coffin. The corpse went into it then all right, but her two feet were cocking out from the ankles down! The dead woman's two sisters when they saw that burst out crying:

'Poor Minnie,' they said, 'bad and all as she was she didn't deserve to have that done to her! You wouldn't do it,' they said, 'to a black Russian.'

And they wanted the husband to postpone the funeral until a proper coffin was made. The husband said:

'No! Delays are dangerous. There's no time like the present!'

So they put the lid on the coffin and brought it to the door. The chief mourners crowded round the front of it, and once outside the coffin was raised on the bearers' shoulders. And the front right-hand man under the coffin, Doherty was his name, took off his hat and held it over the feet. The funeral moved on with dignity and no one was the wiser. Even the parish priest didn't notice anything.

'All right,' he whispered to the men, 'I'll be moving

ahead of ye to the cemetery.'

The people fell in behind the coffin. Then the sidecars, common cars and saddle horses. After a time Doherty's hand, from being in the same position, developed *codladh grifín* and was going to sleep on him, so he took his hand away and left the hat hanging on the feet. People coming against the funeral halted in the middle of blessing themselves when they saw the hat. And you couldn't blame them for thinking they were at the wrong funeral . . . that this must be some great military hero and his hat was being buried with him. At what is called the changing of the bearers, Doherty forgetting himself when he was going, took the hat and left the feet exposed. Lord save us! What an embarrassment this was for the next of kin. They decided to take the short-cut, although the rule is the longest way round to the burial place. It is considered most disrespectful to be in the slightest hurry to get shut of the corpse! Even when the funeral procession gets inside the gate the wrongest thing in the world would be to make a bee-line for the grave. Rounding a bend on uneven ground, and taking the corner too short the legs were taken from under the front bearers and the corpse's feet rubbed against a blackthorn bush. There was an almighty shout from the inside of the coffin. 'Twas Minnie.

'What's itching my feet?' she said.

When the bearers heard that they dropped the coffin. The lid hopped off and Minnie sat up inside the picture of health – two red cheeks on her. The bulk of the people scattered, hid in the wood. Minnie

stood up and walked out of the coffin and she was
the first one home. It was three years to the day
before she got her walking papers again, and I can
tell you that this time the husband took great care
that the coffin was long enough!

Poor Minnie! No tears for her. But if the person
burying was a big loss, like the father of a young
family, the scenes of grief at the graveside would
crack the heart in a stone. Instead of bottling up the
grief inside in them that time people believed in
giving full vent to their sorrow. Didn't certain
women – the *caoiners* – make a trade of going to
wakes and funerals to soften the hearts in the rela-
tions. I saw one of these women moisten the corner
of her apron in her mouth and rub it to her cheeks
to give the impression of sorrow. Oh, the loud wail
of lamentation she made! In no time she had the
women by the graveside sobbing and striking their
hands together, and calling out the name of the dear
departed. And when the young man's coffin was
being lowered into the narrow grave his brothers
overcome with sorrow, surged forward to prevent
it from going down. And as the first shovelfuls of
earth fell, with a hollow sound, on the coffin, oh, my
God a great cry arose, only fading down as earth
falling on earth made hardly any sound at all!

Wing-nuts were all the go at the time. They were
like thumb screws, and very handy they were too,
because you could undo them quickly and the lid
was off in a jiffy. It was the custom then when the
coffin was laid at the bottom of the grave that one

man would go down and unscrew all the wing-nuts and lay them on the lid. This was a nod to heaven that the door was being left on the latch for the resurrection. What great faith!

Now it so happened that a local man died somewhere foreign. This man in his youth had been connected with 'the Movement' and there'd be an outcry if his body wasn't brought home. It was, and when the coffin, foreign made of course, was lowered into the grave a man went down to undo the wing-nuts, only to find that the lid was screwed down for ever! There he was below and couldn't loosen the lid, so he beckoned to those near him. They went on one knee and stuck their heads into the grave and began a whispered consultation with the man below. The question was: would they turn their backs on the old law and fill in the grave, or would they bow to custom? I don't have to tell you what was decided, one of the party got on a saddle horse and scouring the countryside came back with an assortment of screwdrivers, which were handed down to the man in the grave.

In the end the screws were undone and placed in the shape of a cross on the lid, the grave was filled in down to the last shovelful of earth, and the green sods patted into place on the grave mound with the poll of the spade. It took a bit of time, but the people didn't mind once the job was done right. There was only one person who seemed upset by the carry-on and that was the archdeacon. He was muttering to himself about *piseog*s, but he led the final decade of the rosary. That over – old comrades of the soldier that was gone came forward to fire a volley over the grave. Some of these men were so old and crotchety that it was tightening them to direct the guns into the air. So that people dreading mortal injury ducked down and moved back, with the result that Eugene Casey, who was craning his neck to get a view of the shooting was pushed and he fell, bringing three or four more with him, into an open grave and broke his leg! And as a reporter said in the paper the following week:

'Needless to mention this sad occurrence cast a gloom over the entire proceedings!'

The light of heaven to all that's gone and may they never come back to haunt us!

Washing the Cock's Feet

The pooka is a malicious spirit, but not deadly. He can turn himself into any shape, but from what I hear he nearly always appears in the form of a pony. If you are coming home late at night from cardplaying or any other carry-on you wouldn't like your missus or the parish priest to know about; Ah ha! faith, you can meet him! He has the power to coax you up on his back, and then the same as if you put red pepper under his tail, he's off over hedges and ditches, through bogs, brakes and quagmires, from *Poul a' Phúca* to *Gleann a' Phúca*, and from *Carraig a' Phúca* to *Moing a' Phúca*, until finally with the living daylights frightened out of you and your clothes in tatters, just as the cock crows, he'll come to a sudden halt, and you'll go flying out over his head and maybe land up to your neck in a pool of *múnlach*. I'd rather meet Jackie the Lantern than him!

But look at the power of the cock – a small bit of goods. When the cock crows in the morning all things supernatural melt into thin air! The cock is a crabbed bucko. Oh, a fine specimen! And the proud gait of him strutting across the yard on his orange legs! And the plumage of his turned down tail. Did you ever notice the way he'd look at you? First with one eye and then with the other, and when he blinks his eyelid goes from below up! And the red comb like a crown on his head and the chest sticking out!

He'd remind you of Henry VIII – another blackguard!

In our place long ago cocks were suspected of having the power of prophecy. According to the place or the time they crowed, except at dawn, a visitor was expected or someone was about to die in the townland. Whatever was in them they were held in such high regard that they were never killed when they got too old for the caper! They were let go in Merry's Wood, and there were so many old cocks there one time, it was referred to as *Parlaimint na gCoileach*. And a very noisy House of Commons it was too, with the principle motion debated around dawn in the morning!

At that time people used to wash their feet going to bed at night, a custom that is fading away since they got shoes. It seems a big ceremony was made out of the washing of the feet. The biggest pot would be placed in the middle of the kitchen floor and to do it right the youngest male child should wash his feet first. Now the man that had only daughters in the family. What would he do? I'll tell you, he'd take the cock off his perch over the coop, and wash his feet first. Wasn't that a fine healthy piece of paganism!

The King of Ireland's Son

There was a king in Ireland one time and he had no family, only the one son. This morning when the servants got up they found that the field in the front of the house was full of birds of every description. They brought the story to the king that the birds were there, and the king said not to disturb them until he would get up himself.

The king's son was asleep in this room below but, if he was, the talk woke him. He got up and looked out the window, and when he saw all the birds outside he ran for his gun and, firing, he wounded an eagle in the leg. He went out in the field then and the eagle, whatever power he had, motioned to him to sit up on his back. He did, and lame and all as the leg was under him, the eagle flapped his wings, craned his neck and rose up into the air, and flew hour after hour until he landed the king's son in the Eastern World, where it transpired that the eagle's mother was a hag, whatever her son was doing in Ireland in that disguise!

'I'm badly wounded in the leg, mother,' says he, 'but the blackguard that did it is here with me.'

The hag didn't say anything but called the servant girl and told her to put the King of Ireland's son up on the loft over the stable for the night and to give him only a cup of thin beer to drink.

But the servant girl unbeknownst to the hag, gave the King of Ireland's son her own bed, and a damn nice supper which he wanted after the flight. She told him then that the hag had three hard jobs lined up for him.

'Jobs,' says she, 'that are beyond the powers of any human being. But if I can,' she said, 'I'll do my best to help you!'

We'll skip now until morning, and when the King of Ireland's son came down the hag was waiting for him with a tin mug, what we used to call a ponny. She brought him to the door of this gazebo of a house she had and said to him:

'Go down and drain that lake below and look for the gold ring my mother lost there about thirty years ago. Have it for me before the sun goes down in the evening, and if you don't it will be worse for you!'

The king's son went down and he fell to draining the lake with the tin mug until he was blue in the face from it, because for every mugful he'd *taosc* out seven more'd flow in. About twelve o'clock the servant girl brought him the dinner and before he had that finished she had the lake drained and found the gold ring. She brought the ring to him.

'Keep that ring now, yourself,' says she, 'for you'd never know the day or the hour when you'll be sorely in need of it!'

She went home, and in the evening when the sun began to redden the heather on the hill to the east of him, he went into the house and told the hag that he had found the gold ring. The hag didn't say one word to him, but ordered the girl to give him a cup of thin beer and to show him the way up to the loft. But the servant girl, ignoring this, gave the King of

Ireland's son her own bed the same as the night before.

When he came down in the morning the hag was waiting for him with a pitch fork. She brought him to the door and showed him the outbuildings, and told him to clean out the stable where seven hundred horses had been bedded down for seven hundred years. And to look for a darning needle her grandmother lost there more than thirty years before.

'Have it for me,' she said, 'before the sun goes down, and if you don't it will be the worse for you!'

The king's son, God help us, a man not used to that sort of work, went out and began piking dung out the door of the stable, but for every pikeful he piked out seven more came in the window. In no time he was covered in sweat, so he stood nursing the pike until the servant girl brought him the dinner. He sat down and before he had it finished the servant girl had the stable cleaned out!

'Hold out your hand,' she said to him. He did. 'Put that needle now,' she said, 'with the ring and keep it. It might come in handy to you some day!'

She went away and when evening came he too went into the house, and there was the hag inside near the fire. He told her he had found the darning needle, but she didn't say 'huf' nor 'haf' to him, only ordered the servant girl to point out the loft over the stable to the king's son and to give him the usual. The girl did, and when he came down in the morning the hag was waiting for him with a hatchet. She brought him to the door and showed him a tall tree growing in the *bán* outside, and the bottom branch of the tree would be twenty feet from the ground.

'Knock down that tree,' says the hag, 'for there's
a box on top of it, where there's a duck hatching on
one egg, and I want you to bring that egg to me
before the sun goes down, and if you don't it will be
the worse for you!'

He took the hatchet and he went out into the field
and lifting it high above his head with one mighty
blow he sank the hatchet to the haft in the trunk of
the tree. As he drew it out, *slán mar a n-innstear é*,
blood gushed from the tree, and in no time a pool
of blood was rising all round him the way he had to
run out of it, and by the time he got to the high
ground it was twelve o'clock and the servant girl
arrived with the dinner. He sat down and before he
had it finished the servant girl had the tree knocked.
As the tree fell the duck flew away, down came the
box, and the egg fell out of it and into the pool of
blood – if the egg was a *bogán* it was in *brus*! The
king's son's heart came up into his mouth for he
thought the egg was gone for ever, but it wasn't. The
servant girl changed herself into a *madra uisce* and
in the turning of a hand she had the egg up from the
bottom of the pool of blood. She wiped it on her
apron and handed it to him.

'Keep that now,' she said. 'And don't give it to
anyone.'

That night the King of Ireland's son and the servant girl remained up baking and preparing food
for a journey, for they were going to escape before
the sun would rise in the morning. Three times in
the course of the night the hag called out to the king's

son:

'Are you gone to sleep yet?'

To the first question his answer was, 'No.' To the second question his answer was, 'I'm preparing to go.' But there was no answer to the third question for by that time the king's son and the servant girl were on their way back to Ireland. They were going as hard as ever the horse under them could gallop, she up behind him riding *cúlóg*. As the dawn brightened into day she said to him:

'Look behind you and see is there anyone after us.'

He looked back.

'There's two black shadows on the horizon,' he said.

'That's the hag,' she said, 'and the hag's son! Keep going and when they come near us throw the gold ring to them with a drop of sweat from the horse's ear!'

When the hag and her son came up the King of Ireland's son cupping a drop of sweat from the horse's ear and putting it on the ring he threw it back over his shoulder. And when the hag and her son dived after the ring the drop of sweat expanded into a lake and rose up all round them. The King of Ireland's son pounded on and when he was gone another while the servant girl said to him:

'Look behind you and see do you see anyone.'

'Oh God!' he said, 'the two shadows are coming again like the *sí gaoithe!*'

'Quick!' she said, 'throw the needle back over your shoulder!'

He did and as soon even as the darning needle hit

the ground a wall of spikes, criss-crossing sprang up to the heavens.

'We're free of them now anyway!' he said, 'the devil or Dr Reilly couldn't get through that barricade!'

'Give one last look,' the servant girl said when they were gone another bit, 'and see is there anyone behind us!'

He did, but there was only one shadow now.

'That's the hag,' the servant girl said, 'the son is caught on the spikes! Take out the egg now,' she said, 'and when the hag comes up aim it at her heart. If you miss we're finished!'

When the hag came near the king's son half turning in the saddle took the egg in his left hand, he was a *ciotóg*, and he aimed it at her and he hit her fair and square and the thin end of the egg went in through her, and the thick end wasn't long after it. The hag gave one great cry of pain, and she fell to the ground as the soul went whistling out of her. The King of Ireland's son and servant girl, now that the danger was over ambled on at a nice steady pace, and it was dark night when they reached his father's court in Ireland. When they got off the horse she said to him:

'I won't go in with you at all now! It could be a bit awkward having to explain everything. But make me one promise. When they are welcoming you inside don't let your father's little black dog jump up on you and lick your face!'

He said he wouldn't and he went in, and do you know, he was lonesome enough parting with her for he thought she was going to stay with him and marry him. When he went into his father's house that was the great welcome by everyone for him. He sat by the fire and before he realised what was happening the little black dog, trembling with delight at the sight of the king's son, jumped up on his lap and licked his face, and from that second all memory of the servant girl and all that happened in the Eastern World went clean out of his mind!

The servant girl walked on through the dark and when she got tired she went up into a tree. When she woke in the morning the sun was shining. There was a well at the butt of the tree and looking down she could see herself reflected in it. A piece up the road from her there was a forge. When the blacksmith got up he told his wife to go out to the well and bring him a drink of spring – and no word of a lie – the best thing a man could take before his breakfast. The wife went out and when she bent down to fill the jug, she saw what she never saw before a reflection in the well. There were no looking glasses at the time and people didn't know what they looked like, and maybe they were as well off! She thought it was herself – that it was her own image that was in the well! So she threw away the jug and put her nose in the air saying:

'Why should a good looking woman like me be wasting her time drawing water to a dirty old blacksmith!'

And she went off in a daze through the wood reflecting on her loveliness, and firmly intending to find some big town where a raving beauty like herself would be valued!

Away she went. And when there was no one coming to him the blacksmith had to go out himself, and when he looked down and saw the reflection in the well I can assure you he knew that it wasn't himself. He looked up into the tree, and there she was above, a lovely girl smiling down at him. He beckoned to her to come down. She did and went into the house with the smith. And when his own wife didn't come back, she baked and cooked for him and washed his shirt. In return he made for her a silver hen and a golden cock. He was a dinger of a tradesman and the cock and the hen were so well made that they could open and close their beaks and move their legs.

He gave them to the servant girl, and one night she went to the king's house. No one there knew who she was, and she put the little silver hen on the table, and when the people came to watch, she put the golden cock beside the hen. Then putting her hand in the pocket of her apron she threw a grain of oats between them. There was a wild scramble but the cock won. He gobbled up the grain of oats. She threw another grain and another, but it was always the same, the cock got there first and swallowed up the grain.

'Ah,' she said to the cock, 'it is a bad right for you to deny the bite to that little hen. And think!' she said to him. 'And think again! It was that little hen gave the warning and saved your life when the eagle was overhead!'

The king's son was over by the dresser listening

to all this. And I don't know whether it was the sound of her voice or the talk of the eagle that did it. Whichever it was his memory came flooding back to him, and coming over to her he looked into her face. When he saw who he had he put his two arms around her and tightened her into him. She gave him the silver hen and kept the golden cock herself, and they were married the following morning. Everyone that was anyone was at the wedding and I'd be there myself only that same day I was curing a smoking chimney for the Cronin's!

The Cock and the Coop

I remember when I was small they used to keep the fowl in a coop in the kitchen. There was very little in the way of out-buildings at the time, and the more out-offices you had the more rent you paid the landlord, so the hens had to be kept in a coop in the kitchen. They were safe there from the fox. But not the cock. . . his majesty wasn't cooped up. He'd sit on a perch over the door or on the collar-brace – an alarm clock that needed no winding!

The coop made a nice companion piece to the dresser and the settle. It stood, not as high as the dresser, and in outline it would remind you a little of the chiffonier. At the bottom of the coop you had two big compartments. One with nests for the hens to lay in, and the other where the hens could hatch. Then overhead you had the living quarters. Three or four rows with sliding shutters in front. The shutters were made of vertical laths spaced a few inches apart so that when the hens retired in the evening they could put their head out between the laths and take an interest in what was going on, and in that position they'd remind you of nothing in this world only idle women looking out hotel windows in the summer time in Ballybunion!

Hens seem to be forever engaged in conversation. I don't think their musings have ever been recorded. A pity. For there's no end to the variety of sounds they can make from the sad clucks of complaint when they are hungry to the nice satisfied tone they make when they are fed, which can change all of a sudden if a dog rushes into the yard. Standing in a bunch together watching the cock they seem to be talking out of the sides of their beaks and for all we know indulging in a bit of calumny and detraction. Hens have a special tone when they are looking for a place to lay, which bears no relation to the commotion they kick up when they have laid. And of course the hatching hen has a lingo all her own, not very musical like two stones hitting together – cloch cloch – but she can substitute a more appealing call to the chickens when she finds some out of the way piece of food. I think she picks this sound up from the cock, for you'd hear him going on with it when he has a little tit-bit for his favourite wife.

The mother hen has a system of sounds to suit every degree of danger threatening her young. One of these sounds she raises to a frightening note when she sees the hawk overhead. As soon ever as the chickens hear the alarm they disappear or freeze under a leaf or a chaney, and when the mother hen sounds the all clear they come out again as perky as you like. But nothing in the fowl world can equal the lunatic sounds that comes from a hatching hen when her 'chickens' turn out to be little ducks and take to the water. You have then, judging by speech and appearance, a very demented hen!

In many places these articles of furniture, the coop, the dresser and the settle were made of bog oak and that was very hard timber to work. But the people had to use it for the landlords wouldn't let them cut the trees in the demesne woods. A man explained to me once how the local people got the black oak up from the depths of the bog. They would go to the uncut bog early in the morning when the frost was on the ground. And it seems where the log of oak would be reposing, maybe seven feet under the turf, there would be very little frost on the grass over it up. You could see the outline of the log like a shadow on the ground. The men had, as part of their equipment, two long rods of iron. One of these rods was driven down at one end until it met the wood. By driving it down a few times the men were able to determine the width of the log. That done they would leave that rod in position touching the wood, and go off and drive the other rod down through the soft bog to find the length of the log. Then a man would place the end of one rod against his teeth while the other rod would be tapped with a sledge, good and hard, and if the first man felt the vibrations in his teeth that log was all one piece and worth digging up.

Then with a hay-knife they'd cut around the shadow in the frost – they had to work quick before the sun'd rise. The grassy top-sod was removed, and with the *sleán* they cut the turf spreading the sods to dry. The trench deepened and when they reached the log they'd free around it. Because there was no outlet from that trench in a short time it filled with water and the log floated to the top. All they had to do now was tackle a horse to the end of the log and haul it home. When it was dry it was cut with a fakah called a whipsaw into boards and planks for the carpenter, who'd come to the house and make the settle, dresser and coop.

And I could not give down on the amount of ingenuity that went into the making of these articles of furniture. Raised panels in the settle with the rails stop champhered and shaped arm-rests. But it was the dresser that took the cake! A lovely cornice at the top, ogee-moulded with dentils, shelves double-beaded throughout, side and top face-boards with pierced or sunken centres, and two or maybe three overlap drawers in the lower section. If you made it yourself you'd stay up all night looking at it!

They're all thrown out now! Daughters coming back from England or America, not seeing the like over, got rid of 'em. A man told me that he saw a field full of dressers thrown out in the Co. Clare. And he blamed the women too. He said that they went into town and bought plywood furniture with glass fronts to keep the bees off the butter!

The Blacksmith's Wife

Ní phósfhainnse an táilliúirín,
An táilliúirín, an táilliúirín,
Ní phósfhainnse an táilliúirín,
Mar níl aige ach snáthaid!

Agus óró, mo ghoirm thú,
Grá mo chroí forever thú.
Óró, mo ghoirm thú,
Is ní fheadar cé aca a bh'fhearr liom!

Ní phósfhainnse an gabha dubh,
An gabha dubh, an gabha dubh,
Ní phósfhainnse an gabha dubh,
Mar bíonn sé dubh sa cheartain!

Agus óró, mo ghoirm thú,
Grá mo chroí forever thú
Óró, mo ghoirm thú,
Is ní fheadar cé aca a bh'fhearr liom!

[I wouldn't wed the little tailor/the little tailor, the little tailor/I wouldn't wed the little tailor/because he has nothing but a needle!/And bravo/you are the love of my heart forever/Bravo/and I don't know which of them I'd prefer!/I wouldn't wed the blacksmith / the blacksmith, the blacksmith / I wouldn't wed the blacksmith/because he's black in the forge!/And bravo/you are the love of my heart forever/Bravo/and I don't know which of them I'd prefer!]

Ní phósfhainnse an gabha dubh – Ye all know what the lady in the song is saying: I wouldn't marry the blacksmith! Why then I heard of a woman that married a blacksmith, and what's more she came all the way back from America to marry him. He was a good mark for as well as the forge he had a nice bit of land with a good house on it. There was no out and out great love between them, just that he had an empty house and she was tired of America. They got married, a made match, and they made history for they were the first couple from that part of the world to go away on a honeymoon. When they got off the train above in Glanmire station in Cork she says to him:

'They are all looking at us. They know very well that we are fresh from the altar! Is there anything I could do,' says she, 'to make it appear as if we are a couple of years married?'

'Of course there is,' he said. 'Catch hold of the bag and walk on in front of me!'

When they came back from the honeymoon she got in the carpenters and the masons and renovated the outside and the inside of the house. I can tell you that the dresser and the settle walked out the door fairly quick! She put into effect ideas she saw foreign. She made a lovely job of it, concrete paths – you wouldn't see them at all at the time – all around the house outside and a steep concrete path running all the way down to the wicket. With a monkey tree here and a monkey tree there – she was used to the good thing in America, where she was a lady's companion, wintering it in New York and summering it in Spring Falls!

She was full of airs and graces which she tried to transfer to the blacksmith. The poor man! She was always correcting his speech, which might sound all right to you or me, for it was the speech of the locality, full of 'fhots' and 'fhoys' and 'fhuichs' and 'fhayers – my woman!' The man's grammer was putrid! Always saying things like 'she have' and 'he have'. Well, she gave him such a drilling about saying 'he have' and 'she have' that in the wind up, would you blame him, the blacksmith thought that 'have' was a word that shouldn't be said in front of children. And I remember distinctly the blackguards waiting to go into Mass – 'twas the fall of the year – and when they saw the blacksmith coming they said to him:

'Have they the hay cut, up ye'r quarter?'

'Oh, they has,' he said. 'Indeed they has, sure if they hasn't it cut now they'll never has!'

There was a station published for the blacksmith that year. Things were going a bit late because there was a change of parish priest. The way it was the smith didn't mind whether it came or not, but his wife was delighted to have the station in the house, as it would give her an opportunity of showing the priests and the people the improvements she had made, and it would also be a chance to show them all the curie-fibbles she had brought back in the trunk from New York. She made up her mind that the day of the station was to be a big day and she wasn't going to have such an important occasion ruined by her husband's awkwardness, so training was the answer.

For weeks before the station the poor blacksmith hated to see the sun going down in the evening, for it meant home to night school! And when he got inside the door of the lovely new house he had to get out of his old duds that were dirty from the forge, scrub himself from head to foot, and get into what he called his conversation clothes. She put a lot of stress on speech: 'Yes father' and 'no father' and 'I beg your pardon, father'. Being the man of the house he would have to have his breakfast in the room with the priest after the station Mass. So she showed him how, in smiling fashion, to fix the chair at the head of the table for the priest, and for God's sake not to pull it from under him as he was going to sit down!

'Have your manners,' she told him. 'Make sure everything is up to the knocker. Pass the sugar and pass the milk, and no coarse conversation,' she said, 'in the presence of the priest.'

She didn't want him saying things like: 'Excuse me, dear father, the butter is hairy; the dog and the cat slept in the dairy!'

'None of that,' she said to him. 'And use your serviette and don't have drops of tea falling from your moustache! And take the spoon out of your cup while you are drinking, and don't have it going into your eye while you are talking to the priest!'

Being the man of the house he would have to go

down the steep path to the gate the morning of the
station to greet the P.P. when he got off the sidecar.
Before he'd go to work in the forge his wife brought
him down a few times to show him how to do it
properly. He was to stand there showing no agita-
tion and when the priest got off the sidecar to extend
his hand and say:

'Good morning, dear Father!' Then he was to look
around and with a controlled laugh add: 'Fall
already. We won't feel it now to Christmas!'

He didn't want to say 'Fall already' because he
hadn't heard it around. It was a proper term she
told him and used in New York to describe the
autumnal part of the year. It was the coming thing
she persuaded him and that he could put his bottom
dollar on it. He was doubtful. He didn't think it a
homely expression, and he used to be saying it to
himself to get used to it. 'Fall already. Fall already!'
When he got up in the morning before his prayers
he'd say 'Fall already!' Even when the forge was full
of customers all of a sudden he'd stop hammering
the hot iron on the anvil and looking up at the roof
he'd say 'Fall already!' until the people thought he
was going out of his nut!

Every evening when he came home from the forge
the table would have a new cloth on it, and each
evening she would introduce him to a different item
of cutlery, spoons for this and that, a little silver
tongs for the loaf sugar, knives crooked and straight
and pieces of table-ware, glassy salt cellars and a
butter cooler with a roof on it!

The night before the station he washed the footpaths all around the house. And the steep path down to the gate. . . bucket after bucket of water he sloshed it down. Then as he was at the gate and there was no one looking he extended his hand. This would be the final practice,

'Good morning, dear Father.' Then he looked around and laughed as directed. 'Fall already! We won't feel it now to Christmas.'

He went back up to the house. They went to bed, himself and the returned Yank, and whatever happened that night, maybe the clock didn't go off in the morning or the cock didn't crow, whatever it was they were only barely down in the kitchen and when they looked out the window there was the parish priest's sidecar drawing up below at the wicket gate. The blacksmith stuck his legs into his shoes and ran out the front door. Lord save us! There was a fierce fall of frost the night before and the minute he hit the icy path the two legs were taken from under him and he came down with a crash on his backside and went skeeting down to the gate! From the sitting position he extended his hand and said,

'Good father, dear morning. What a day you came! God, I broke my bum in the fall. I'll feel it now till Christmas!'

It Snowed that Night

There were these two poets and they used to go every year to the winter fair in Kenmare to buy two cows for the tub. When the deal was done they'd tie the two cows to the lamp post and go into the pub, where they'd spend the day and portion of the night arguing, insulting people they didn't like and exchanging verses. When they'd come out bye an' bye they wouldn't be cold but the two cows would be perished. When they'd rip the ropes off their horns the cows'd gallop off to get the blood back into circulation.

Now, it so happened one year that the poets bought two black cows, and when they got out of the light of the town, the night was so dark and the cows so black, that the poets couldn't see a splink. There they were with two ashplants running up and down, hether and over, in gaps and out gates after the cows. They could only go by the sound, so when they heard anything they'd draw with the ash plants and were hitting one another as often as not.

They spent the night on the road, up bohereens and into fields, and when it brightened in the morning they were driving two animals before them! Not their own I'm afraid. Two rangey bullocks belonging to some farmer in the Roughty Valley. By the time they had the bullocks restored to their rightful owners, by the time they had gone around to all the schools and made public the fact that the cows had strayed, and by the time they had found them they swore they would never again get into such a mix-up of an adventure if they could at all avoid it.

Time moved on and the winter fair in Kenmare came round again, and neighbours were surprised to see the two poets late at night in a public house and they *maith go leor!*

'It is none of our business,' the neighbours remarked among themselves remembering the fools the poets made of themselves in the dark the year before. 'Yerra let 'em at it!'

Drink or no drink you couldn't be ikey enough for poets. They got an inkling they were being talked about so one of 'em got up and sang,

We don't give a *tráithnín* about darkness,
Be it blacker than nature allows.
We're prepared for it this time, my buckos,
We've purchased two handsome white cows.

It snowed that night!

May Morning

I often heard it said that on May morning before the sun would rise people used to go out to the wood and bring in branches of greenery, hazel, holly, elder, and rowan, and they'd come chanting through the fields:

> Samhradh, samhradh, bainne na ngamhna,
> Thugamair féin an samhradh linn!
> Thugamair linn é is cé bhainfeadh dínn é,
> Is thugamair féin an samhradh linn!

[Summer, summer, milk for the calves/we brought the summer with us/we brought it with us and who'd take it from us/we brought the summer with us.]

They'd bring the green branches into the house, hanging a big one maybe on the outside of the door, and then when the rising sun'd light up the kitchen they'd greet the summer with:

> Come sit you down on a chair of silver,
> Come sit you down on a chair of gold!
> You are welcome, my brother with us to linger,
> It is long since we saw you and we are tired of
>   the cold!

If people were seen doing that now, they'd be committed, we have got so anglified!

We used love to be sent out that morning to pick flowers for the May altar. You'd see the young calves calling for their breakfast. They'd give only a small bellow first so as to let people know they were in the receiving line. Then if no notice was taken of that, they'd increase the volume until you could hardly hear the hens clucking, the cock crowing or the dogs barking turning home the cows from the macha! Looking over a ditch that morning you might see a hare sitting in a field, and even though you ducked down, he'd have a sort of a notion you were watching him, and rising on his haunches and craning his neck he'd take stock of his situation. No need to turn his head, for he can see behind as well as before, and his hearing is so acute that at the breaking of a withered kippen he's off like the *sí gaoithe*. Like Balor of the Evil Eye the hare is often connected with the superstitions of May morning.

There was a certain man and even though he had a big bane of cows he had nothing worthwhile in his churn. He couldn't make out what neighbour was doing the damage until he was told to watch his herd May morning before the sun would rise. He rode down at break of day, a couple of dogs at this heels and concealed himself. Nothing unusual, only that he had a bit of trouble keeping the dogs quiet for there was a hare in the macha moving around among the cattle, and he couldn't believe his eyes when he saw the hare sit down on his little cor-righiob and milk a cow!

He let the dogs go and galloped after 'em. Talk of a chase and many is the turn the dogs knocked out of that hare, one of 'em got so close to the hare he took a piece out of his shank. Even so they lost the hare, but they didn't lose the scent for it brought 'em to the front door of a house. The man got off the horse and looked in the window and there was an old woman inside and she bandaging her leg where the dog had taken a skelp out of it! The Lord save us!

She had to be read over. I forget what priest was there at the time, but they said when he went into the house smoke was seen coming out of it. I can tell you the Latin cured her and the man's profit came back to him and he had no trouble making his churn after.

Butter-making like everything else connected with farming was a risky operation, and you could never be sure that it was going to turn out right, until the cream would crack and looking down you saw a fine lump of gold sitting in the bottom of the churn. The churn was made once a week and anyone passing by was expected to pause, bless the work and lend a hand to show that there was no ill will. In other words put the size of his head in the churn, for that was the amount of profit he could take with him if he didn't give a hand.

You couldn't take fire out of a house on May morning. And another time you couldn't take fire out was during the churning. There was a grand-uncle of mine, often I heard it, and he was going the road east to Knocknagree and he came to a place where they were making the churn. Well, how was he to know that! He went into the house to light his pipe – he had no matches. As he was going out the door

the son of the house came before him and wanted
to take the pipe out of his mouth and spill the red-
dened tobaccy on the floor. Now my grand-uncle
might have to walk two miles before he'd get another
pipeful so he hit the son a clatter and knocked him
against the dresser. Then the father came with the
tongs, and as true as heaven he'd have opened my
grand-uncle with it only at that very minute the
woman of the house came out of the dairy and clap-
ping her hands she said:

'The churn is made!'

So full of apologies they let my grand-uncle go.

As far as we know dairy farming was ever the way
of living in this barony, and the return from the sale
of home-made butter was the principle income of
the people in those days, so if anything went wrong
with the cattle they were in a bad way. There were
no vets or department help or advice when animals
got sick. There was no one to turn to but the cow
doctor, a man born with the 'gift', the likes of Johnny
Con. And another thing, you see, there was a wide-
spread belief in remote places that disease was a
result of some evil influence, and one way to get rid
of it was to give it to someone else! So that if a man's
cows slung and continued to sling, to be clear of the
misfortune that man might go at dead of night and
bury the lost calf or the cow's 'cleaning' in the
neighbour's land!

Was it any wonder that people, frightened by the
paganism of bad neighbours, used to resort to driving their cattle between bonfires on Saint John's
Eve, and was it any wonder that they had to shake

holy water on the young crops during days of roga-
tion. One man described that to me as Christian
Paganism.

Archdeacon Godfrey went a long way towards rid-
ding our parish of such superstitions. Before he came
no man would cut his hair on Monday. There was
no luck in Monday's work, and the old people'd go
out of their minds if they saw you throwing the hair
cut off your head into the fire. Every rib of it had to
be gathered up and put outside in a hole in the ditch
to await the resurrection. Don't you think but there
will be some hairy old lads knocking around that
day!

Archdeacon Godfrey was death down on the
piseog. No incantations or spells, supernatural
observances, *dúirt sé dáirt sé* or pagan *cogar mogar*
as far as he was concerned. You'd have to tell it in
confession if you turned back from a journey because
you met a redheaded woman on the road, or if you
made a *snaidhm na péiste* over a cow with a colic,
or if you passed a child under a donkey's belly as
you recited the Lord's prayer, and then put him sitting on the cross on the ass's back to cure him of
whooping cough! When the archdeacon heard of
such carry-on he used to say:

'Why are we sending missionaries to the swamps
of New Guinea when paganism is rampant at home?'

And it was! Not in our part of the country where
the people were a little more enlightened. But this
way to the north of me toward the Shannon evil
abounded! Usedn't they put eggs in hay! It seems
you could do great damage with a *glugger*! I heard

from a man's very own lips. Twelve winds of hay they had, he said, and when they drew the hay into the shed, they found two eggs three feet down from the top in every wind. He said his father nearly went out of his nut. They made a fire in the haggard and they boiled the eggs, and he said it was the devil to boil 'em. Then he said they perforated the eggs, steeped 'em in paraffin oil, burned 'em and buried the ashes. It was all to no avail. Everything went wrong that year. The cows slung, the cock got the croup and a litter of bonavs they had never grew! They drove black hair out through 'em as long as your finger. They were more like badgers than bonavs. The little pigs began to bark and turned very vicious until they had to be destroyed. I tell you the egg is something of a mystery!

But to go back to Johnny Con. He was in great demand when I was young for curing people and animals. He was said to be the seventh son of a seventh son, born on Good Friday and baptised on Easter Sunday, so where would it go from him.

'How would you stop a cut bleeding, doctor?' says the archdeacon to him with *searbhas* the morning of a station.

'I'd put a cobweb to it,' says Johnny.

'And what, might I enquire, are the curative properties of the cobweb?' says the archdeacon.

'Isn't it well known, father,' says Johnny, 'that the spider was ever highly thought of. Didn't he spin a web around the manger so that Herod's soldiers couldn't get into our Lord when he was small!'

Johnny had an answer for everything. Although

the Holy Ghost didn't descend on him until fairly late – he was shaving before he was confirmed! And the bishop, questioning the confirmation class, couldn't help noticing the size and the rakish appearance of Johnny, so he asked him did he know what was forbidden by the ninth commandment. Johnny said he did. The bishop was doubtful so putting it in very plain language he said:

'Would it be all right for you now to make love to your neighbour's wife?'

'*T'anam 'on diabhal*, my Lord,' says Johnny. 'Why would I do a terrible thing like that and the country full of young, lovely girls!'

But what made Johnny the talk of the parish was one Sunday during a sermon on company keeping. The archdeacon was very vexed, and when he came to the part about the young couples going up the lonely bohereens, he raised his voice to a shout and a young girl that was leaning over the gallery fell down, only, mercy of God, to be caught by the legs by her aunts above, but they weren't quick enough. Her clothes fell down over the girl's head. A gasp went up from the congregation, and the archdeacon looking at the people said:

'Any man who turns his head and gazes at this woman in her nakedness will be struck blind!'

And Johnny, covering the left side of his face, said:

'I'll chance one eye!'

> A charming creature he espied convenient,
> And she sadly playing a melodious tune.
> She far transcended the Goddess Venus,

And her appellation was the Cailín Fionn!

That was one story about Johnny, but a story he used to tell himself was in great demand when weather was bad and people were down and out.

Daniel O'Connell and the Colonel from Battersea

The Cork butter market, in its hey day, was the biggest in the world and it was said to grease the axel of the entire British army. You'd go up Shandon Street to it. It was like a bee-hive, well a *cruiceog* for it was round, with all the activity of buying and sampling and weighing and grading and testing. There was a man then with a fakah like an auger which he'd drive into the firkin and when he pulled it up, he had a cross section of what was inside. He'd run it across his nose tasting it with his tongue – what a job to have! – to see if it was all of equal quality and that there was nothing rancid at the bottom, and you were paid according to his pronouncement. The butter market made Cork, gave plenty of work and made the merchants rich. And one of those merchants went up for election one time; the opposition said he wouldn't get in, but his followers said he would,

'For,' says they, 'we'll graze his arse with butter and we'll skeet him to the top of the poll!'

It wasn't a landslide but he slipped in!

Butter was going to Cork from every corner of Munster on horse back long before the roads were made. Squads of men would set out from as far south as Cahirciveen, and one horse would be loaded down with food for the journey. Later on when the coach roads were developed the car men came. They were a hardy breed of lads, and my own great grandfather was one. And they'd take as much as a horse and cart could carry of butter to the city and they'd bring back goods to be sold in the local shops when they were coming.

All that long journey could not be done in a day, so the butter men had special houses, in places like Carriganime, where horses and men could rest the night. These were houses where stories of the past and the present were exchanged, and every man would bring home a head full of news about the heroes of the day.

Daniel O'Connell was over in London at the time and he was staying in this hotel called the Royal Victoria. He was having his dinner one day surrounded by a lot of rich people. They didn't think very highly of Dan, for it was well known that Daniel O'Connell was on the side of the poor. Wasn't it the poor people that put him into parliament the first day. And another thing, at the time Dan used to defend people in court that broke the English law, and because of that, I can tell you, he had very few friends in the city of London. During the course of the meal Dan, maybe he had a sup in, had occasion to go out the back. And while he was outside what did this fellow that was sitting alongside him do but spill the contents of a packet of white powder into Daniel O'Connell's cup! The servant girl was there and spotted it, and when Daniel O'Connell came back she said:

'A Dhónail Uí Chonaill,
A dtuigeann tú Gaoluinn?'
'Tuigim go maith,' duirt sé,
'A chailín ó Éirinn.'
Agus ar sise:
'Tá nimh id chupán a leagadh na céadta!'
'Más fíor san, a chailín,' duirt sé,
  'is mór é do spré-sa!'

[O, Daniel O'Connell/do you understand Irish?'/'I
do, and well,' he said,/'O, girl from Ireland.'/And she
said, 'There's (enough) poison in your cup to stretch
hundreds.'/'If that's true,' said he, 'your dowry will
be great.']

   And she told him then in Irish, Irish is handy
abroad! She told him that she saw this fellow, *seana-*
chornal ó Bhattersea a bhí ann, putting white powder
into his cup. With that there was a great commotion
outside in the street, shouting and cheering. Queen
Victoria that was passing down, so all the quality
ran over to look out the window. When there was
no one watching him what did Daniel O'Connell do
but exchange the cups, so when this old lad from
Battersea came back he took the cup with the poison
in it and drank it down. He died on the spot! Thanks
be to God that Dan came safe out of it. Daniel O'Connell wiped his mouth and wrote out a cheque for the
servant girl. He went out then taking the air for himself. He was going along when this *giobhlachán* came
after him jeering him and singing a disparaging
rócán,

A Dhónail Uí Chonaill M.P. mar eadh!
Taoi i bhfad ó do mhuintir san áit seo.
Téir ar ais go hUíbh Ráthach,
Dos na prátaí is bláthach,
Is fág an áit seo do na huaisle!

[O Daniel O'Connell M.P./you're a long way from your people in this place/go back to Ivearagh/to the spuds and the buttermilk/and leave this place to the nobles.]

Daniel O'Connell eyed the singer and enquired, *'An Ciarraíoch tusa?'*

'Ó sea,' he said.

'Duine de mhuintir Coffey?' says Dan. The Coffey's were of the travelling class.

'Ó sea,' he said. *'Is mise Dydeo.'*

['Are you a Kerryman?'/'I am,' he said./'One of the Coffey's?' says Dan./'Yes,' says he, 'I'm Dydeo!']

'I know your clann very well,' says Dan. 'I know ye all. Often I saw ye on the road from Castleisland down to Cahirciveen. Tell me this, Dydeo. Who put you up to sing that piece of *ráiméis* for me?'

''Twas the owner of that hotel over there, the Royal Victoria. "Sing anything you have handy in Irish for Daniel O'Connell," says he, "and you'll get money from him!"'

'Oh, you'll get money all right,' says Dan, 'but it won't all come from me! Come over here!'

And he brought Dydeo into a barber's shop where he got the man to give him a good clip and a shave and to powder him up. Then he took Dydeo into a

haberdashery. 'Formal Wear' was written over the
door, where Daniel O'Connell fitted Dydeo from the
skin out in what was the height of fashion at the
time. A tall silk hat, a cravat, a cut-away coat, patent
leather shoes and when he came out carrying a walking cane and wearing a 'glass eye' Dydeo looked a
real gentleman!

Then Danel O'Connell says to him:

'There's a fist-full of money for you now, and go
back, down to the hotel, find the owner and rent a
room from him for the space of a week. Be sure to
bring me back a document signed by the owner to
show that all is legal. And come here,' says Dan to
Dydeo tutoring him up and showing him how to
walk with a nice measured pace. 'Be very careful of
your speech. Don't open your mouth over big when
you're talking and keep the tone a little bit down
out of your head! Say you are from Siam and that
your wives are coming this evening!'

Aren't they broadminded in London! Imagine
bringing a squad of wives into a hotel in Tralee.

Off with Dydeo, and do you know, when you're in
the right clothes it is easy enough to fool people.
Dydeo came back in no time with the document
signed and the room ready for occupation. Dan ran
his eye over the paper.

'That's fine,' he said. 'Keep it safe. Where's the
rest of the clann? I don't see them around.'

'There's only the one place they'd be now,' says
Dydeo, 'and that's above in Dirty Dick's in
Cricklewood.'

'Off with you up so,' says Dan, 'and get all your

friends, men, women and children to come down to the hotel and take over that room you are entitled to.'

Away with Dydeo up to Cricklewood and when he went into the public house above of course he thought no one would know him in the fine clothes. *Mo léir* when he walked in the door they all stood up and burst out laughing.

'Come out from under the hat,' they said, 'we know your legs.'

He told them of the plan and they collected up the pots and the pans, the canteens and the tin, the clippers and the timber hammers, and men, women and children came down in a body, down to the hotel. They went in the door and up the stairs and into the room, and they weren't a second inside when they began clouting tin, and the like of it for a *clismirt* was never heard before or since in the city of London.

The quality were having their dinner downstairs and the noise knocked such a start out of them that the food went down the wrong passage. The owner ran up the steps when he heard the clitter, and when he beheld the state of the room and saw what was happening inside, he rushed over to the window and called a squad of police that was passing outside. Now, it was a man called Sullivan, one of the black Sullivans from between Listry and Lisaphooka, that was over the police in London at the time. The minute he walked into the room and saw the Coffeys he knew who he had, and going over to Dydeo he said to him in a very threatening tone, 'You'll g'out of it!'

'I wo' not,' said Dydeo, 'g'out of it!'

And Sullivan shoving his jaw into Dydeo's face said to him again, 'You'll g'out of it now!'

'I wo' not,' Dydeo told him, 'g'out of it now or any other time. I've this room rented for a week, as I have a contract to make saucepans for the British army. Take a look at that paper,' giving the agreement signed by the owner to Sullivan. The policeman ran his eye down the paper and as he read it his face fell. Then turning to the owner he said, 'This document is pure legal. They can't be evacuated for a week!'

The owner went into a reel and began kicking the wall with the dint of bad temper.

'I'll be ruined,' he said, 'by that time. The quality are moving out already!'

'Well,' says Sullivan, a man well up in the matter of bribery, 'if you want the custom of your lords and ladies gay you know what to do,' and he winked at him and gave him the nod, so the owner drew Dydeo aside and asked him, would he evacuate for a consideration and Dydeo answered that that depended on the size of the consideration! The bargaining began and they went from a pound to two pounds to four pounds and Dydeo and the clann didn't put a foot outside the door until everyone got a fistful of notes. Then they gathered up the pots and the pans, the canteens and the tin, the clippers and the timber hammers and went down the stairs and out into the street. There was Daniel O'Connell outside on the flags waiting for them and a big *clab* on him laughing!

Dydeo looked at the money and then at the heavens saying, 'God direct us where will we go, Cricklewood or Castleisland?'

'There's a better kick,' says Dan, 'off the stuff in Castleisland.'

So they hit Fishguard and took the tub to Cork singing at they went:

> *Ó Oileán Chiarraí mo mhuintear-sa,*
> *Ach i nGort an tSléibhe a rugadh mé,*
> *I bpoll fé'n chlaí go moch san oích'*
> *'S narbh dheas an féirín dom mhamaí mé!*

[My people came from Castleisland/But I was born in Gort a'tSléibhe/in a hole under a hedge early in the night/And wasn't I the fine gift for my mother!]

Ulick, Aeneas and Andy

Máire Bhuí Ní Laoire the poet was joined in butter with the Callaghans. Poets don't get up too early so that Máire was always running with the night, and it was dark one evening when she was going over to Callaghan's with her little keeler of butter on her head. When she was passing Gugane lake, whatever look she gave, the waters of the lake had parted and she saw the sun shining in the land below, the people working in the fields, the cars going down the road, and she could hear the birds singing and the bell ringing in the chapel. She knew that if she had a piece of steel to throw into the lake the waters would remain parted and she could walk down there and converse with the people below and find out what sort of a story they had.

She remembered that there was a steel tip on the heel of her shoe, so she put the keeler of butter on the wall of the little bridge. But when she bent down to rip the lace she had to take her eyes off the lake, and when she looked up again the waters had closed in. She went up to Callaghan's and told them of the beautiful vision she had seen and how sad it was that the waters closing in had prevented her from going down to meet the people.

'Do you know,' says Timmy Callaghan to her, 'wouldn't the story be a lot worse if the waters closed in while you were below!'

At that time, because of the small holdings, you'd

have three or more families joined in butter. The produce of one farm would not be sufficient to fill the firkin, which was a tub-like container sent to the butter market in Cork. Each family would bring their share of butter to your house this week, to my house next week and so on. I don't know how they kept track of the individual contributions to the firkin. It must have been a good system for it was said that families joined in butter never fell out.

Packing the firkin was a job for the women. They'd clear the kitchen table and on it they'd wash the butter and re-wash it in lovely spring water. Then with butter spades they'd blend the produce of the different farms, for there could be a variation in the colour according to the amount of clover in the grass. And there's nothing worse than streaky butter! That done they'd add a touch of salt to keep the life in it, and a dash of saffron to heighten the colour. When the firkin was packed and covered in muslin, the lid was put on and the hoops fastened down.

If there was any butter beyond the household needs left over the women would make it into little bricks shaped with the butter spade which had a flowery design cut into the face, and these prints of butter were put sitting in a fresh cabbage leaf and given to a poor person who had no cow of his own.

It would do your heart good to see the women working together. Young women walking barefoot on the wet floor, their clothes loose on them in the height of summer. Fine bouncing women with black curly heads and they full of their pickey! God help the man that'd stray into that company, moreover, if he was of a shy disposition. They'd take the trousers off him. And they'd laugh enough at him!

There were these three men, Ulick, Aeneas and Andy, fine big men with round faces like a full moon. They were always drowsy looking with heavy lids coming down over their eyes. They had enormous appetites and when they were full they'd fall asleep on the back of a harrow. They were likeable, easy going, sociable lads that would do anything for a laugh. One day in town they went into a shop in Henn Street and asked them for a yard of milk. The shopkeeper didn't turn a hair. You could be asked for anything in Killarney! He just dipped his finger in the churn and drew a line of milk a yard long on the counter.

'There ye are!' he said.

'Thanks very much,' one of them says. 'Roll it up and put it in a paper bag and we'll pay you for it!'

Brothers they were, Ulick, Aeneas and Andy. They had no mind for girls and some people said that it was from the father they brought that caper, for he didn't get married until he was over sixty. The father was an enormous size of a man. When he went to Wales in 1901 the Welsh government wouldn't let him down the mine in case he would block the shaft! 'Did you come over in one piece,' they wanted to know, 'or were you assembled here?' He got drunk one night in Cardiff, and on his way home to his lodgings he fell into a cut stone horse-trough and fell asleep, his legs cocking out below and his head above. The water in the trough covered him from his neck to his knees but he didn't wake. That night the water froze making himself and the stone all the one piece. Even that didn't wake him! The tram cars in the morning, they used to make the devil's own clitter, woke him up. He got to his feet, noticed nothing, and made his way to a public house where he stood with his back to a roaring fire. Well a few minutes after he was the most surprised man in Europe when he heard the crash behind him. It took ten Welshmen to lift the horse trough out in the yard!

His three sons, Ulick, Aeneas and Andy went to the bog one day to cut a *sleán* of turf. Ulick was on the top sod, Aeneas benching and Andy spreading. The day turned very hot, and after the dinner they went into the *cois*, lay down on the *fionnán* and fell asleep. There they were lost to God and the world when three young lassies came racing down the bank full of devilment as all young girls used to be at the time. When they saw the three boyos below they jumped down into the *cois* and pulling three stems of *ceannbhán* they began to tickle Ulick, Aeneas and Andy under their noses until they woke them up!

And whatever came over Ulick, Aeneas and Andy, don't ask me, maybe it was the time of the year, they fell head over heels in love with the young girls. What am I talking about! They followed them home every step of the way and told the girls' mother, that not one foot would they put outside the door until they got a promise of her three daughters in marriage. The old lady was huffy enough about it, saying that she had something better in mind for her daughters than to be marrying them off to farmers, and small farmers at that.

'And they are three refined ladies,' says she, 'that never wet their fingers only upstairs eating biscuits and looking out the top window!'

But the three daughters said they'd sooner Ulick, Aeneas and Andy than if three lords came jangling their spurs to the door for them. The old lady had to be satisfied with that, and the arrangements went ahead for the big day. That night the mother called in the three daughters and said to them:

'I have no fortune to give ye only one purse of gold but as that is too small to divide it between three, I'll give it all to whichever one of ye will make the biggest fool of her husband after ye are married.'

We'll skip now until the day of the wedding. The three lads kept awake long enough to say 'I do' in the chapel. At the wedding dance that evening, after a feed of roast goose washed down with an ocean of drink, when Ulick, Aeneas and Andy hit the hay they went into a deep coma! God help their wives! In the morning the lady who was married to Ulick when she couldn't wake her husband thought to herself, as there was nothing else doing, that she might as well have a shot at winning the purse of gold. She took the scissors and cut off his hair and beard. Then she laddered him and shaved his head and face so close that the draught woke him! And when he opened his eyes, after the feed of *poitín* the night before, he was as drunk as when he went to bed.

'Who are you?' his wife said to him.

'I'm Ulick,' he said.

She took the looking glass off the wall and held it in front of his face. He came out of the bed and when he saw his bare frame, long and lanky and his shaved head in the glass, looking for all the world like an Aran Banner on top of a walking cane, he said:

'Well, that's not me whoever it is!'

'And what are you doing here?' she wanted to know. 'Clear off out of this and don't come back until you find the man of the house!'

So off with him – isn't drink a fright – and he shouting, 'Anyone here see Ulick! Anyone here see Ulick!'

Around dinner time the second daughter that was married to Aeneas tried to waken her husband. Not a gug out of him! She put her ear to his chest. Not a sound. If his heart was beating it was keeping fairly quiet about it. That he was warm was the only sign that he was alive! So with an eye on the purse of gold she went out next door where there was a card of a woman living, and the two of them got a habit; there used to be a habit in every house that time. With the scissors they cut the brown shroud up the back and fitted it nicely around the man in the bed. They joined his hands in prayer, entwined the rosary beads around his fingers, lit a couple of candles and put the word out that he was dead. Indeed herself went into mourning, wherever she got the black dress!

Later that same day the youngest girl that was married to Andy – having spent the whole night and part of the day in bed with him in the hope that he'd wake got tired of it and went out to see what the day was doing.

Like everyone else she heard the sad news and rushed back and began to shake her husband saying:

'Wake up! Wake up! Your brother is dead!'

'Which one of them?' says he, rising out of the bed.

'Aeneas,' she told him. 'He went class of a sudden too, so they're burying him in a hurry. Put on your clothes and straighten out or you'll be late for the funeral.'

'My clothes,' says he. 'The Lord save us! Didn't I throw my shirt and all my old duds into the fire thinking now that I was married I wouldn't have to get up anymore. What'll I put around me?'

'It is a poor head,' his wife said, 'that there isn't a plan in it! Come up here to the kitchen to me.'

He went up to her in his nakedness, and she melted down a basin of lard and rubbed it well into him all over! She went out then and she brought in the pluckings of a black and white goose and shook the feathers on the floor.

'Roll yourself in that now!' she said.

He did, and when he got up he wasn't like anything that anyone ever before saw, and the only thing you could say about him was that he wasn't naked! Off out the door with him. He was late, for the funeral had left the house. He ran after it, and when the mourners looked around and saw the apparition behind, they dropped the coffin and ran. The coffin falling woke up the man inside! The lid flew off and when the 'corpse' stood up and saw Andy in the feathers the legs gave under him with fright and he sank down into the coffin again.

Aeneas and Andy had hardly time to recognise each other when a man ran up shouting:

'Anyone here see Ulick? Did you see him, holy father?' thinking, when he saw Aeneas in the habit, that he was a friar!

'Aren't you Ulick?' they said. They were sobering up now. 'Yerra, you're Ulick,' Aeneas said, 'we'd know you boiled in porridge!'

There they were looking at each other and wondering how they became so transmogrified. Was this what marriage had done to them? Then all of a sudden realising the trick their wives had played on them, they got into a tearing temper, and decided there and then that they'd go up to their mother-in-law's and wreck the house on her for landing them with three such mopsies of daughters. But when they went in above their wives were sitting inside before them, so they said nothing!

'There they are now, mother,' says the daughters. 'You see the cut of them, that's the result of the caper. It would be time for you to be delivering your judgment!'

The old lady stood up and she wasn't long about it. Looking at Ulick she said, 'Samson lost his hair!' Looking at Aeneas she said, 'Lazarus is risen from the dead!' And looking at Andy she burst out laughing, 'The purse of gold,' she said, 'goes to my youngest daughter. It is a simple thing to make a fool of a man but it takes a bit of ingenuity to make a goose of him!'

The Biddy Boys

There was another custom at the time called going out in the Biddy! We young people used to go in parties from house to house on St Bridget's Eve collecting money, and in return we'd sing and dance in the kitchens. With the proceeds we used to buy shop bread and jam, and if we could rise to it a half tierce of porter for an all night dance which would be held before Lent began.

All the fun was in the dressing up for the Biddy and we went to great extremes to conceal our identity. Women used to dress up as men, and many is the sedate old farmer, sitting in a neighbour's kitchen, spotted his Sunday suit dancing around in a set. His daughter, Mary that'd have it on! She'd hear about it after. A very forward young lady might get into her father's long johns, and if there were a few family heirlooms like a cut-away coat and a caroline hat to go with it she would look something going around in the hornpipe figure of the set dance.

A lot of straw was used in the disguise. You'd see Biddy boys in straw capes and straw puttees, and back around Beaufort they had specially made mitre-shaped straw hats to wear over the capes and puttees. When they'd burst into a house on Bridget's Eve you'd swear they came up out of *Lois an Phúca!*

We used to wear high fiddles – hallowe'en masks which were coming into the shops at the time – or we'd cover our faces with the screen off the window.

You could see out and breath in through this lacey fabric, and the alteration it made to the physiognomy was truly remarkable.

Every party had a *brídeog*. There is some doubt as to who this effigy was supposed to represent. We thought it was St Bridget and the priest thought it was St Bridget, but then again you'll hear another person say that the custom of lugging the *brídeog* around was in the world long before St Bridget saw the light of day.

To make a *brídeog* you'd put straw around the handle of a brush bulging it out below and above. Doll it up then with a skirt and a blouse, and with a carved turnip for the face set in a head shawl and fixed to the top of the handle. What would give a damn nice effect would be to scoop out the inside of the turnip and put the butt of a lighting candle into it. Every party going along would have a musical instrument, or maybe two, but if they couldn't rise to that they'd dyddle or they'd play on the comb.

When we came to a house, and if we were admitted, we'd take over the kitchen. The person with the biddy – the *brídeog* – would stand by the fireplace, the musicians by the dresser and the rest would crowd on to the floor. As the music struck up we'd take a partner saying:

'Come on, shake a leg!'

Mhuire Mháthair, the pounding the flagged floor'd get, and if any pots or saucepans came in the way they went flying under the settle. When the set was over, order would be called for a step dance or a song. Then the biddy boy would collect whatever money the household was inclined to give. Not a great lot, but by setting out at nightfall and covering a fair bit of ground we'd get a good few bob together for the ball night.

Local people who became a bit enlightened, or should I say anglified, were always ashamed of those customs, and the clergy considered the *brídeog* a mockery, an insult to St Bridget. They discouraged the practice and put an end to the porter nights. And the young people had only themselves to blame for that, for those biddy balls, as they were known, were often held in houses without proper supervision. As a man said to me, 'With all the drink and everything, Ned, the thing could develop into an orgy.'

And he was right, partly right anyway, for you had fellows there half-plastered and couples *mouzing* up along the stairs, in the room and in the linny! Then you'd have a modicum of men who can't get women, they'd be up to some other devilment. They might go out and tie the door from the outside, put a coarse bag over the chimney, and as the house filled with smoke shove red pepper under the door. Pandemonium would follow, sneezing, coughing, cursing, swearing and as the music came to a halt the stairs would become alive, and the room and the linny, for as we all know there is no vexation in the world to equal that of men interrupted in love-making. They would swear vengeance on those responsible and by shoving a small fellow out through the window to untie the door, they'd rush out and it would be open war with the crowd outside. And I remember one night one section took cover behind the rick of turf and the opposing party behind a pit of turnips. Sods and swedes came flying through the air. It was like Dunkirk, which gave Archdeacon Godfrey any God's amount of ammunition for the following Sunday's sermon. As if the man hadn't enough to contend with already!

Mary O'Shea's Story

Every year in the springtime a woman used to come
to our house to give my mother a hand cutting the
sciolláns. A worn table knife she'd use with a rag
around the handle to give it a nice comfortable grip.
And whatever knack she had she's knock as many
sciolláns out of a twenty-stone bag of spuds as
another woman wouldn't knock out of a buttful.

Myself and the other small lads in the family had the
job of keeping the *cliabh* at her left hand side full of
potatoes, and then to draw away the *sciolláns* and the
sceamhacháns as they came from the knife. A *sciollán*
is a wedge of potato having at least one good eye from
which the young plant will grow, and a *sceamhachán*
is what's left of the spud when the *sciolláns* are cut
from it. There'd be a box of lime handy and we'd
have to put a shake of that on the *sciolláns* to keep
them from bleeding. Another job we had was to keep
the different varieties apart. You had a fair share of
varieties in those days some of which you wouldn't
hear of at all now. You had the 'Puritan', an airly,
the 'Champion', the 'White Rock', the 'Up-to-date',
semi-airlies, the 'Irish Queen', the 'May Queen', the
'Epicure', the 'Flounder' and the 'Blue Ball'.

But to get back to my story, the woman's name
was Norrie. A tidy, compact little *dailc* of a woman,
fresh for her age, well dressed, no finery and with a
very correct form of speech, if she found herself in
the right company, keeping the words a degree or

two down in the throat to give the effect of polite-
ness, but when she was cutting *sciolláns* she spoke
like the rest of us.

She was a good hand to put a face on any story
she heard in her travels. When the tea'd be wet bye
and bye, operations would come to a halt, and as
often as not the conversation between Norrie and
my mother'd turn to whatever those subjects are
that women don't consider suitable for broadcast-
ing. Norrie's eye would roll in our direction and my
mother would tell us to, 'Go out there and see is the
cow in the cabbage and don't be watching every
word that comes out of our mouths!'

Small and all as we were we wouldn't be natural
if this order didn't make us all the more eager to
know what was being said. So by diving under the
settle or running above the room door we'd often
hear what wasn't meant for pen or paper. And I
remember the same as if it was yesterday Norrie
saying to my mother on one occasion:

'*Cogar i leith chugham, a stór,* and I'll tell you
something that'll put the cap entirely on what you
were hinting to me a while ago. We went to Wether's
Well one time, we used to go there paying rounds
when my husband got the rheumatics. We used to
go to Lady's Well in Ballyheighe too but he found
Wether's Well more beneficial. We used to stay with
a man named whose name I forget, I think he was
from Clare and his job was giving out the back milk
in the creamery. He was married to a local woman,
as big a talker as himself, and when there'd be a
crowd in the night of the rounds the place'd be like

a university.

'One night the talk turned to *piseogs* and the capacity certain people had in the old days for doing evil. According to the man's wife there were two women and they had a fight. Neighbouring women can fall out over many a thing. Fowl trespassing, geese and ducks wandering, it is easy enough to put a match to the powder where this type of livestock is concerned, and the fight developed into a black feud. Now, one of the women was expecting an increase in the family. Her time came but if it did nothing happened. She went here and she went there but doctors couldn't do anything for her. Don't you think but hadn't she a nice story of it!

'At that time there were very knowledgeable individuals going from place to place. They were known as the Connacht women. One of them bowled the way and she hadn't her leg inside the door when the woman of the house gave her a full account of her trouble.

'"And it baffled the world," she said to the Connacht woman, "for it should be here long 'go whatever is keeping it!"

'"Tell me," says the Connacht woman, "have you an enemy?"

'"I have," she said. "Myself and my neighbour, are no friends."

'"I'll go into her now," says the Connacht woman, "and she will ask me if I have any news."

'"I'll give you money if you can do anything for me," says the woman who was expecting.

'"I won't take any money from you," the Connacht

woman said. "Not for a while anyway."

'She went to the neighbour's house not pretending a bit and the neighbour's first question was, "Have you any news?"

'"I haven't then," the Connacht woman said. "I haven't any news, only that I was into this house over and there is a fine baby there after the night."

'"Are you telling me the truth?" says the neigbour turning very tetchy.

'"I am, eroo," says the Connacht woman. "They have a great time over. They'd give me whiskey if I'd drink it but I didn't. A big belter of a baby that's there, God bless it."

'The neighbour's face went every colour and going up under the chimney she brought down *a leithéide*, like some sort of effigy with a shawl around it.

'"*T' anam 'on riach*," says she. "What did I want this thing above here for if what you say is true. No child could be born to her while that was up the chimney. Bad luck to it, I mustn't have put the right spell on it!"

'And she took the rag doll and threw it into the fire. Well, it blazed up like carbide and when the last shred of it was burned the child was born to the woman over! And a fine boy he was too, with his front teeth up and down to him.'

There was a knot out of one of the boards of the room door. I put my eye to the hole to see how my mother was taking it. I think she believed every word of it, for lifting her eyes to heaven she said to Norrie:

'Isn't there an awful lot of badness in the world!' And of course there is too!

The Archdeacon, His Clerk and His Curate

The old people held that you should talk about a priest only for as long as you could hold your finger in the fire.

In Victorian times Archdeacon Godfrey would never lift his eyes from his book if you met him on the road. He was a fine block of a man and never wore an overcoat or had a fire in his room, and signs on it, he lived to be nearly ninety years of age. He was an arch-Tory and so well in with the powers that be in London at the time, that he could save a man from the gallows if he wanted to. He thought the sun, moon and stars shone out of the royal family, and no Sunday would pass that some time wasn't given over to praying for one of the crowned heads of Europe. He was kept busy for, at that time, kings were so plentiful you could hardly throw out the feet water at night without wetting one of them.

Archdeacon Godfrey was a cut above the commonality, coming as he did from big people. You'd nearly want a permit to talk to him, and when he came to the stations he'd always have his breakfast on his own in the parlour. Even the curate wouldn't venture down, and if he did the archdeacon wouldn't throw a word to him. No one was allowed down only his retriever. He was as standoffish as his master. If you looked at the dog he'd turn his head and look

at the ceiling. He sat there by the table waiting for
the occasional morsel which the archdeacon dropped into his open mouth.

The archdeacon wore a full beard, a tall, silk hat
and a swallow-tail coat with two buttons at the back
as big as the cover of a tea pot. And sitting up on
the wing of the sidecar going into town with a watch
chain glistening across his middle, if he didn't look
the picture of grandeur call me Davey! Patey Barry,
the parish clerk that used to drive the archdeacon,
Patey would take a drink when he was out, but he
wouldn't go too far seeing the responsible position
he had. One day in town he ran into a wedding party
from Gortamikeerie. Barry's mother was from there,
and the Gortamikeeries brought him into Washout's
and treated him to plenty of porter. When he came
out he was staving, legless; he was so full that if he
leant sideways he'd spill!

He made his way to the courthouse where he had
left the sidecar with the horse tied to the railings.
The archdeacon was there before him, his wing of
the sidecar down and he sitting up reading his bre-
viary. He never turned his head, being a bit sulky
at the delay he had waiting for the parish clerk.
Patey Barry ripped the horse and leaving down his
wing of the sidecar sat up and drove way. Everything
went fine and when they came to the bottom of the
Pike Hill the horse slowed down to a walk going
against the rising ground. Then with the nice even
sway of the sidecar, and the fumes of the drink rising
to his brain, Barry nodded off thinking of his
mother's people, and the horse, when there was no

one urging him on, his pace got slower and slower, and his head sank lower and lower, even the archdeacon nodded a little bit as his eyes got weary of reading the holy scripture.

Up the hill they went like that until they got to the top and then Barry woke up, and noticing the slow pace of the horse he did a thing no human being should do, he drew a lash of the whip. And the horse in dreamland, and not expecting it, made one bounce forward so that Archdeacon Godfrey was catapulted off the wing of the sidecar and describing, what one eye witness called, a parabolic curve, landed on his head in the gutter of the dyke. Barry drove on, never missed his passenger, and when he arrived outside the chapel there were people there waiting to go in to early confession, and they wondered what could have happened to their good priest. The next car on the road picked up the archdeacon and when he arrived he was in a ferocious temper and facing over the parish clerk he said, 'Barry, you are drunk!'

Barry looked at the archdeacon's silk hat made into a concertina on top of his head, he looked at the side of the swallow-tail coat caked in mud and winking at the crowd he said, ''Tis aisy to see whose drunk, father!'

Of course the archdeacon never touched a sup in his life. Even so, age overtook him and in the end it was the curate was running the parish; and when I was young the people were never done talking about the difference between the two men. The curate was only a couple of weeks in the parish when it got out that he was an easy man in the confessional. His only comment on the most hyronious of misdemeanours was, 'Three Hail Marys and say a prayer for me, my child.'

One Saturday night the archdeacon and the curate were hearing. . . their two boxes facing each other across the floor of the chapel. There was a huge crowd for confession the same night, the last chance of making the Easter duty. Three quarters of an hour went by and no one had darkened the door of the archdeacon's box. He got a bit curious and getting to his feet he parted the purple curtains and looked out, and there he saw half the parish around the curate's box. He uttered an 'Ahem,' for attention and said, 'Is there a slope in the floor or what!'

Unlike the archdeacon the curate was never out of the people's houses, drinking tea and playing cards. Royalty wasn't bothering him. Not at all. He'd be down to the inch every Sunday evening his coat and collar off kicking football. When the men were busy during the week and he had no one to practice with he trained the archdeacon's retriever to bring back the ball to him. In time he built up a great team, and the Sunday they were in the final, that's the Sunday you'd have a short Mass! He'd scorch through the Latin, no sermon, only a tight warning to the congregation to be sure and be down at the field. This message would be given when he had rattled off the announcements. Then picking up a sheet of paper from the corner of the altar the dead would be prayed for in a hurry:

'Your prayers are requested for the repose of the

souls of Hannah Finn, Johnny Deegan, Jimmy Connolly and Lizzie Horgan whose anniversaries occur at this time.'

Then as he rolled the sheet of paper into a ball he would continue, 'May their souls and the souls of all the faithful departed rest in peace!'

And as he came to the final word, he'd toss up the ball of paper and meeting it with a flying kick put it out between the two pillars of the gallery!

* * * * *

They went the lower road I came the high road, they crossed by stepping stones I came over the bridge, they were drowned and I was saved, but all I ever got out of my storytelling was shoes of brown paper and stockings of thick milk, I only know what I heard, I only heard what was said and a lot of what was said was lies!

Glossary

a leithéide – its like, the like of it
An Domhan Thoir – The Eastern World

bán – an untilled field, a bawn
Biddy – form of Bridget
Biddy Boys – young people collecting money house to
    house on St Bridget's Eve
bogán – a soft-shelled egg
bohereens (bóthairíní) – little roads
bonavs (bainbh) – piglets, bonhams
brídeog – ceremonial image of St Brigid
brus – bits, crumbs, dust
burying – being buried

Cailín Fionn – fairhaired girl
caoiners – mourners
Carraig an Phúca – The Pooka's Rock
ceannbhán – bog-cotton, cotton-grass
ciotóg – a left-handed person
clab – open mouth
cliabh – basket, creel, pannier
clismirt – noise, din
cnavshawling (cnáimhseáil) – grumbling, complaining
codladh grifín – 'pins and needles'
cogar i leith chugham a stór – I'll whisper you this, dear
cogar mogar – hugger-mugger
cois – shelter of turf bank
corrighiob, ar a – on her hunkers
cruiceog (coirceog) – beehive
cúlóg – the pillion seat on a horse
curie-fibbles – bric-a-brac

dailc – smallish, thick-set, little person
Dia linn! – God be with us!
Dia linn is Muire – God be with us, and Mary

dinger – a person outstanding in his/her field
dúirt sé dáirt sé – gossip
dyddle – make port a' bhéil or gob-music

eroo (arú) – yerra!

fionnán – coarse mountain grass

giobhlachán – a ragged person
Gleann an Phúca – The Pooka's Glen
glugger – addle-egg
gug – sound

high fiddles (aghaidh fidilí) – masks
hyronious – outlandish, outrageous

keeler (cíléar) – a tub used for cooling liquids
kippeen (cipín) – little stick

linny – lean to
Lios an Phúca – The Rath of the Pooka

macha – field in which cattle slept at night in summertime
madra uisce – an otter
maith go leor – (in drinking terms) nicely
'Mhuire Mháthair' – Mary, mother of God
Moing an Phúca – The Pooka's Marsh
Mo léir! – Alas!
mouzing – courting
múnlach – liquid manure, putrid water

os cionn cláir – laid out (as of corpse)

Parlaimint na gCoileach – The Cocks' Parliament
pickey – high spirits
piseog(a) – charm(s), superstition(s)
poitín – home-distilled (illicit) whiskey, poteen
poll – back

Poul an Phúca – the Pooka's Hole
pooka (púca) – hobgoblin
put the cap entirely on – round it off

sceamhacháns (sceamhacháin) – peelings or waste potato
    after seed eyes have been removed
sciolláns (sciolláin) – potato set, small potato
seana-chornal ó Bhattersea a bhí ann – he was an old
    colonel from Battersea
sharoose (searbhas) – bitterness, sarcasm
sí gaoithe – fairy wind
skelp (sceilp) – a piece
slán mar a n-innstear é – let everyone be safe where it is told
sleán – turf-spade
snaidhm na péiste – serpent's knot (part of a charm to cure
    colic in cattle)
spifflicated – confused with the weight of drink
splink (splinc) – spark, glimmer

ráiméis – nonsense
rócán – an old song
room – parlour

t' anam 'on diabhal – your soul to the devil
t' anam 'on riach – the devil take your soul
taosc – to drain
tierce – barrel
tráithnín – dry grass-stalk, a wisp of straw